REBORN EVERY DAY

By Fida Fayez Qutob & Dalia Qutob

with Adnan Ghaleb Husseini

Published by Fida Qutob & Dalia Qutob

Copyright © Fida Qutob & Dalia Qutob 2023
2023 Cover Design and Layout © Helen Braid

The authors have asserted their moral right under the Copyright Designs and Patents Act, 1988, to be identified as the authors of this work.

All quotes contained in this book are the copyright of the authors.

All rights reserved. No part of this publication may be reproduced, stored in retrieval system, or transmitted, in any form or by any means without the prior written permission of the publisher, nor be otherwise circulated in any form of binding or cover other than that in which it is published and without a similar condition being imposed on the subsequent purchaser.

A CIP catalogue record for this book is available from the British Library.

REBORN EVERY DAY

The route to your best inner self

AUTHORS' NOTE

We all have power over our minds. Once we shape our minds, we can easily reshape our lives.

It begins in your mind and ends in your life!

Find the passion to create a better version of yourself every day.

The best things in life always begin with YOU!

Fida Fayez Qutob & Dalia Qutob

Fida and Dalia Qutob are proud to partner in this project with Adnan Ghaleb Husseini. Adnan is 14 years old with a special spark! He has partnered with Fida and Dalia in other projects as well. At just five years old he was the spokesperson for one of their children's stories!

Adnan displays a level of creativity, wit, and analytical thought that is quite rare at this age.

Adnan's message: "Dream, but have the courage to chase your dream."

Write it in your mind;
Every day is a new beginning.
Believe it in your heart;
Every day is your best day!

You are reborn every day.

Create a fresh
start and a happy
ending each day.

HAPPY MORNINGS!

When you wake up in the morning,
just think: I am reborn again!

You are reborn every day. You can create
a fresh start and a happy ending each day.

Celebrate yourself every day.
After all, you attract what you feel.

Every morning, awaken your self-worth
before stepping into your day.

Allow your soul to breathe.

FOLLOW YOUR DREAMS

Happy people fill their days
with actions, not reactions.

Make up your mind to be happy!

A smile is the best outfit you can wear!

CREATE YOUR OWN STAR

Maybe you look up in the sky
and don't see your star.

Trust yourself ...You can
create your own star.

You too have wings,

Just spread them and fly.

YOU!

You create your own energy.
You can be the spark.

Don't go looking for the light…

It is YOU who possess the light!
Let your aura be bright.

So why don't you reinvent yourself
and start a new journey?

Just remember,
Any door can open,
but only if you knock first!

*Everything is
a state of mind.*

Load your character!

LET YOUR HEART SING!

Be who you want to be
in your dreams.

Happy because...
Happiness is appreciation in action.

Positive because...
Positivity is the best diet for your mind and body.

Charismatic because...
Charisma is when the soul salutes the souls!

Inner peace

...is an
irrevocable agreement.

TAKE A CHANCE!

It is time to know that you can make
your way even if the path is crowded.

Take a moment and think;

Only if you take a chance,
will you have a chance.

That fear of making a mistake
is the ultimate mistake.

Because…

We fail only when we stop trying.

We need to try until we stop failing.

So, don't turn one failure
into a life sentence!

Success is never met by chance,

only by choice.

A WISH WITHOUT WILL IS HOMELESS!

Don't ever take a U-turn.

Confront one challenge
with a bigger challenge.

Rejections are nothing but catalysts.

Limitations are simply illusions. Ignore them.

Turn that wall into a door!

You will soon find out that will is the
invisible force that makes things visible.

Alter the strategy but not the target.

Omit later from your vocabulary.
There is no better time than now.

REACH FOR THE SKY

Vision is a glimpse

into the invisible.

PATH TO NEW BEGINNINGS!

Sometimes a wish goes unfulfilled
because God has a better choice for us.

Obstacles can reveal a stroke of luck.

Be aware that exits are
just doorways to new beginnings.

And success consists of a bunch of failures.

KEY TO SUCCESS!

If you aren't looking for success,
you will never find it.

Soon you will realize that

'Reason' is the reason for success!

In fact, success is the total
sum of vision and mindset.

But when it comes to self-worth,
always overestimate.

LIFE SPEAKS TO YOU!

What life conceals; Karma reveals.

Start watching the signals. Life speaks to you!

Pick up on the omens.

IQ is the parameter of light in the mind!

HOPE IS A MANTRA
WE HAVE TO REPLAY
EVERY DAY!

Don't focus on that slammed door.
Just walk through a new one!

When things are not going your way,

Don't call it a bad day.

Struggles generate power

And wisdom is the product of wounds.

It's only when the hurt is over that
we realize we gain from pain.

KEEP GOD'S LIGHT AROUND YOU!

There are times in life when
you wonder why and how?

You will get the answer once you
feel God's presence around you.

Whatever your dilemma is, choose the truth.

Honesty is God's voice within you.

Conscience is an ongoing dialogue with the self.

Faith allows you to win battles unarmed.

Religion is about opening hearts
not closing minds!

LOOKING IS EASY. SEEING IS DIFFICULT!

When you look, see; when you hear, listen.

Listen to the mute statements
and shaky voices.

You will find that the shakiest
voices might be the sincerest ones.

When you listen, feel.

If you can't feel the light,
you will never see it.

Intellect is when brains

meet hearts!

EDUCATING HEARTS!

No matter how many degrees we obtain,

    Educating hearts triumph
    over educating minds.

    And self-education offers
    the highest degree of education.

    Just remember that

Every teacher is a student,

Every student is a teacher.

Guide others,

*but don't leave
yourself lost!*

ROOM FOR KINDNESS!

There is always room for kindness.

Kindness strengthens
the muscle of the soul!

He who lifts, gets lifted.

Karma justifies success.
Karma also justifies failure.

Unkindness is being unkind to oneself.

Lifting spirits is the best workout routine.
Be the star in someone else's sky.

STRIVE TO HAVE A CHARACTER THAT LASTS!

Character is defined by how you react when anger defeats you.

Anger dissolves immunity.

It leaves one with a wounded spirit.

Don't forget that it's mean
to say things we don't mean!

When anger is at your door, inhale;

Patience is a silent prayer.

Sometimes a smile is the best apology.

Don't let that stranger

reside within you.

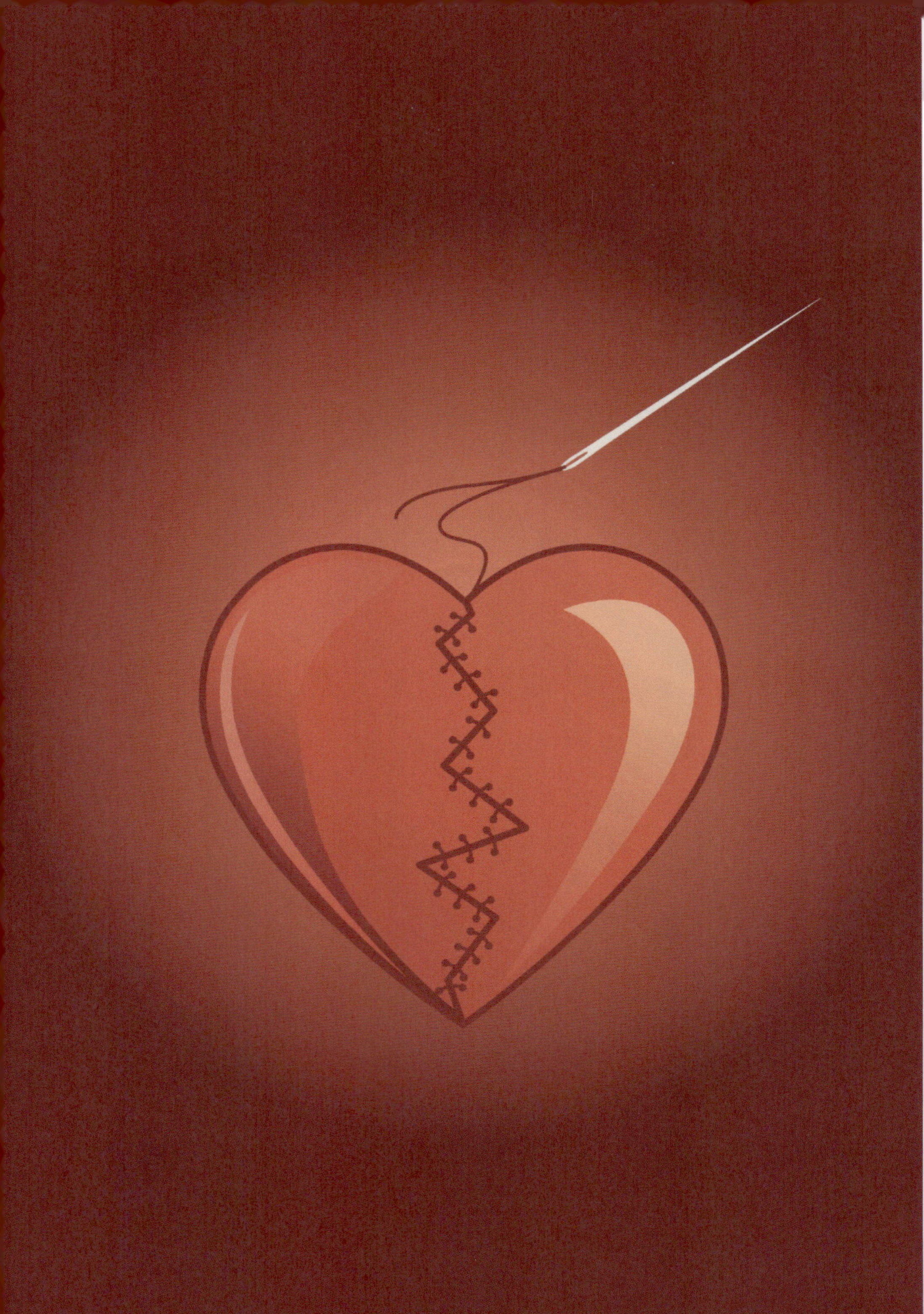

REWARD YOURSELF!

As we search for happiness, we tend
to forget that it starts from within.

Forgiveness is rewarding oneself.

Don't let that scar reinjure you every day.

It takes courage to fight.
It takes more courage to reconcile.

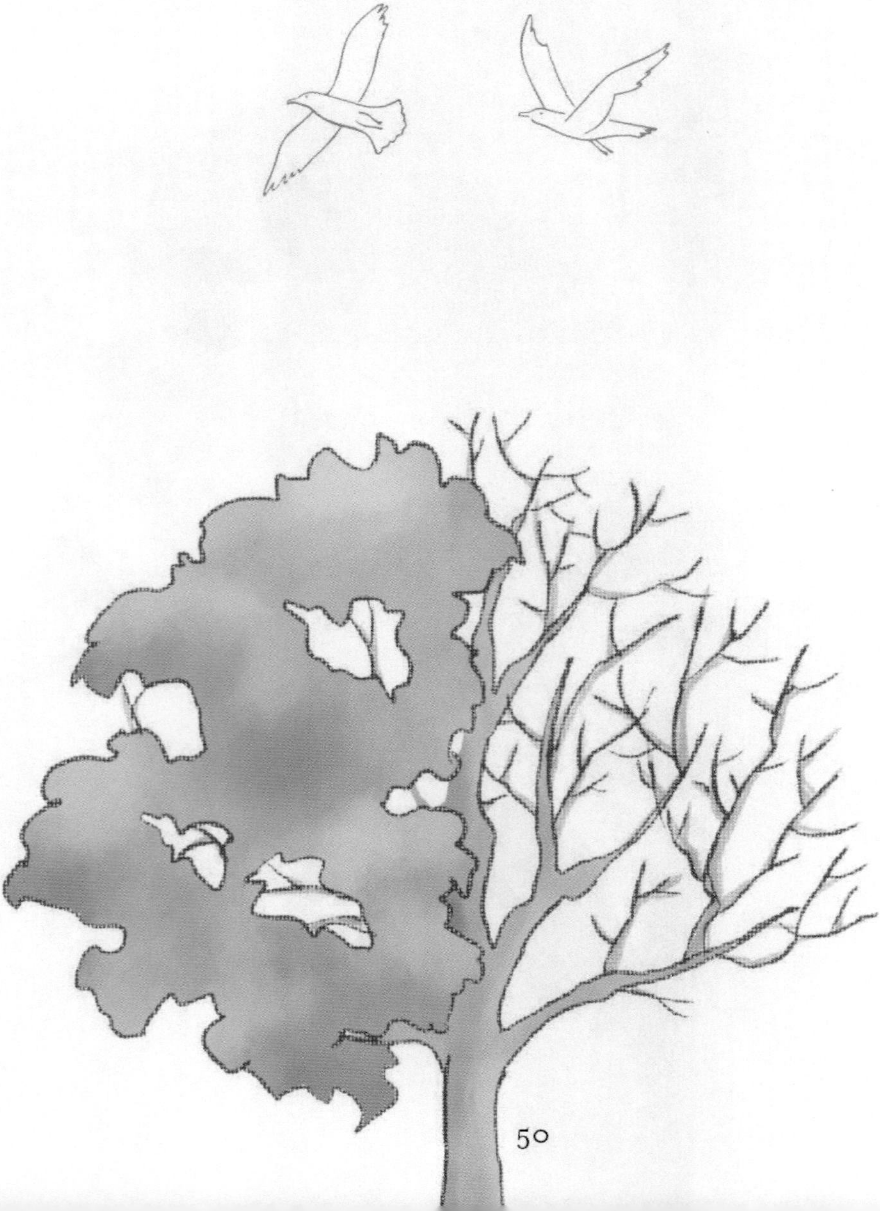

THE POWER OF BELIEF!

Believe in thyself. You live what you believe.

The echo of your thoughts
is louder than you thought!

Changing thoughts… changes lives.

Let self-confidence be your best soul mate.

Insecurity clouds the brightest sunshine.

Worry blocks energy; sedate it!

YOU TRANSMIT ENERGY!

Be the sunshine within the clouds.

Positive vibes are the
highest in frequency,

The wonder of positivity is
that it gives your deeds spirit.

Just remember that
words have smiles, too!

The aura

is the reflection of the soul.

LET YOUR SOUL SHINE!

What you believe, life perceives.

When the soul shines, no darkness is feared.

May I remind you not to leave that child behind.

Children love with all their hearts...
dream with all their minds...
forgive with all their souls.

Let's be children forever!
Let's live in their spirit together.

GIVE A CHANCE

The moment you give someone a chance,
you clear your own path.

And when you empower someone else,
both of you become lifted.

Be generous whenever you can.

Generosity is measured with time,
not money.

And the most precious gifts
are the gifts felt with the soul.

Whatever you give away comes back
to you in the most splendid way.

The wealth of the philanthropist only
appreciates and never depreciates.

Humanity is one simple answer
to thousands of complicated questions.

Make an impact. Make a profound impact!

Take a journey and
wander within oneself.

The day you find
your true self, you will
never be lost again.

SPIRITUAL RENDEZVOUS!

Meditation is the Pilates of the mind.

Only when we understand the philosophy of silence, can we better understand the words.

If inner peace is the cause,
then outer peace is the effect.

Make an appointment with yourself.

Self chats are the deepest.

Sometimes silent answers
are the most fluent ones.

Explore oneself.
Dive into the Zen Cosmos.

But just beware,

Your thoughts can be heard by the universe.

Unwind to let your spirit unbind.

Relax and exhale worry.

Liberate your mind.
Visit a spiritual destination.

LOVE ON PURPOSE!

Family · Friends · God · Life · You! · Music · Sea · Sports · Yoga

Let me warn you,

If you forget to love yourself,
others will love to forget you.

Live for a purpose,
love on purpose.

Don't sit there counting the moments.
Make the moments count!

'Love calms the energetic

and energizes the calm'

- Adnan Ghaleb Husseini

OUR RECIPE!

One day you will realize that respect is the magic ingredient for self-esteem.

When self-respect walks out, disrespect walks in.

Pour some appreciation!

People who belittle are usually bitter.

True wealth is appreciating what you have!

THE SECRET OF POSITIVITY!

Feed your thoughts!

Thoughts can heal.
Thoughts can also contaminate.

Negativity is the pollution of the soul.

Surround yourself with positive people and they will find a solution for every problem.

But if you surround yourself with negative people they will find a problem for every solution.

Negativity is contagious. Eradicate it!

SET YOURSELF FREE!

The most dangerous wars
are the ones declared upon the self.

Nobody can build your prison except you.

Nobody but you can dictate your life story.
Be your own author!

Prisons with invisible bars
are the most wicked ones.

Set yourself free!

SUCCESS GUIDE

In the equation of life,
values are the only constant.

Intellectual battles are the only legitimate battles.

Manners survive the fiercest disputes.

Integrity is a contract with yourself
you can never annul.

LIVE LIFE AS A GIFT!

Remember the lesson, not the failure.

Being at peace with yourself
will be your best masterpiece.

Your thoughts dictate your life.
Screen them!

When thoughts talk, the universe listens.

Compose your life story,
you will soon live it!

HAPPY NIGHTS!

I hope you never allow yourself
to go to bed broken!

Go to bed with a dream,

Dream before you sleep.

Dream is a vital sign.

Don't forget that entrepreneurs
are persistent dreamers.

Fall asleep with a new hope in your heart.

Tomorrow is a second chance. Use it!

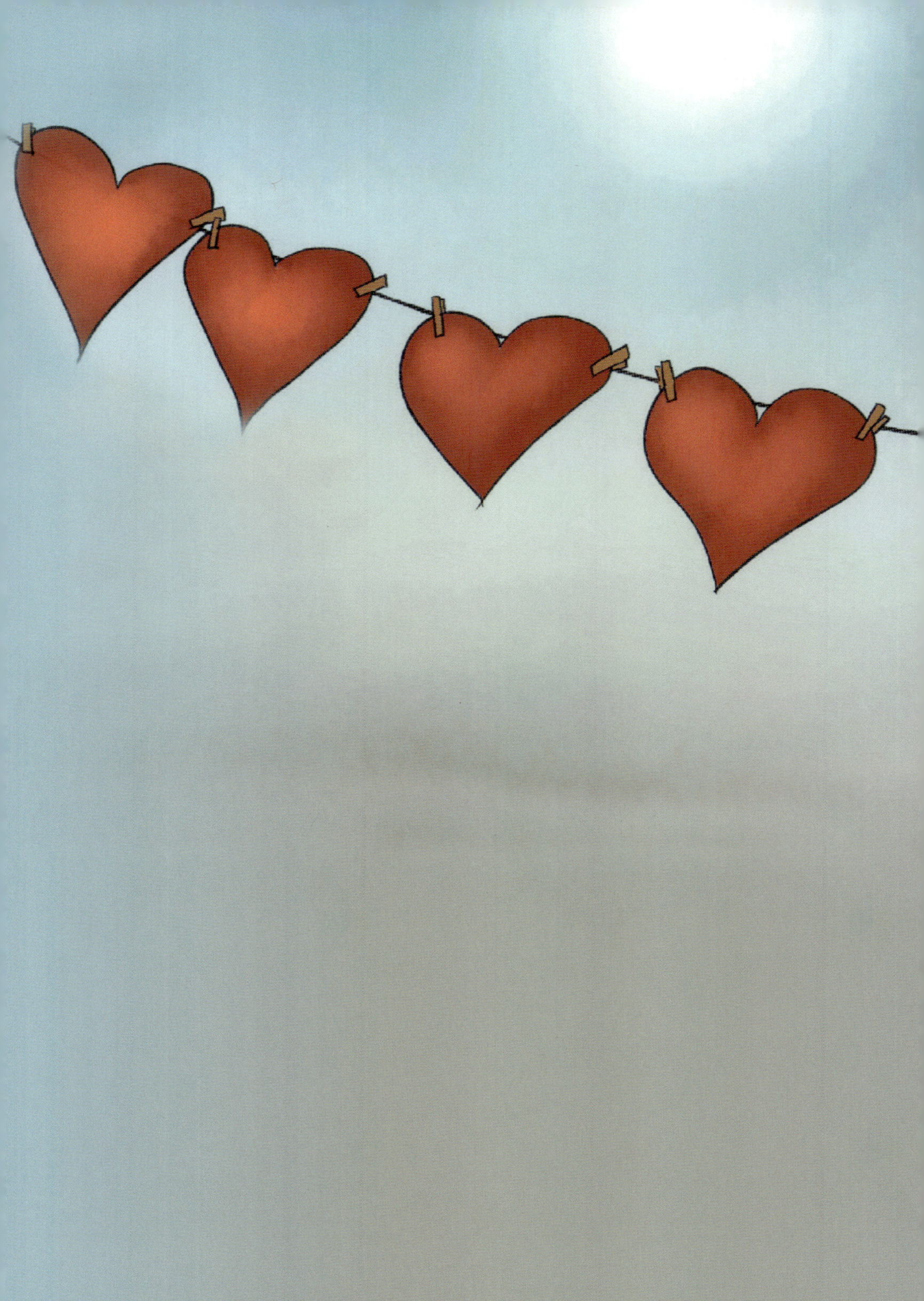

Tomorrow is a second chance. Use it!

Printed in Poland
by Amazon Fulfillment
Poland Sp. z o.o., Wrocław
18 May 2023